Sea Bones

by Bob Barner

chronicle books·san francisco

Wonderful creatures live in the sea.

Vertebra

Caudal fin

Caudal ray

Rib

Pelvic fin

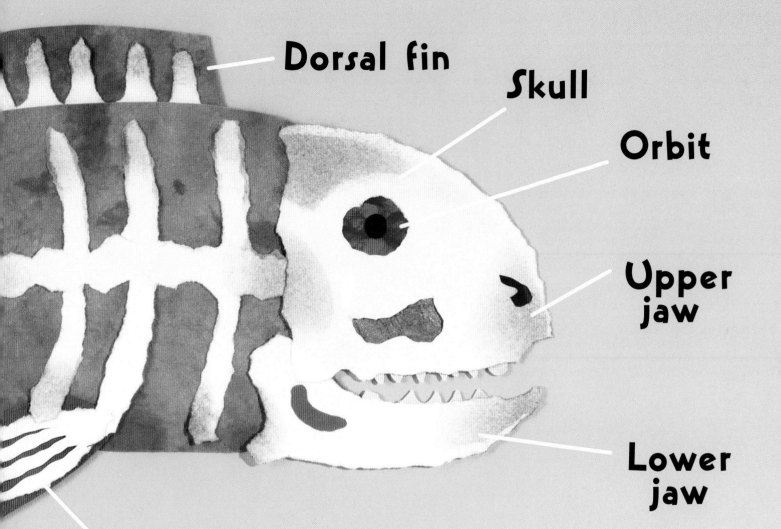

Dorsal fin

Skull

Orbit

Upper jaw

Lower jaw

Pelvic ray

Skeletons support the organs and muscles of many creatures in the sea. Most fish have a skeleton made of bone. Because it is inside their body, it is called an endoskeleton. Some animals, like lobsters, have a hard shell on the outside of their body called an exoskeleton.

The largest animal on Earth, the blue whale, can grow to be 100 feet (30 metres) long. It has an endoskeleton with 176 bones. Whales have a backbone, which makes them vertebrates. The blue whale eats tiny shrimplike creatures called krill.

And some have bones like you and me.

A coral reef sparkles on the ocean floor.

A coral reef is home to many animals. Some of the animals, like crabs, are invertebrates, which means they do not have a backbone. Crabs have an exoskeleton. Hermit crabs do not have bones or their own shell. They live in the used shell of another animal. If the shell gets too small, they choose a new one and move in.

Made from the skeletons
of those that lived before.

A coral reef is alive. It is made of thousands of tiny animals called coral polyps. The reef grows on the hard skeletons of dead coral. It takes thousands of years for a reef to form. Animals are attracted to coral reefs because they offer a home, protection, and food.

There are animals without bones

Jellies have no bones and no brains, and they go wherever the ocean currents take them. The lion's mane or hair jelly is the largest jelly at up to 8 feet (2.5 metres) wide with tentacles 120 feet (36.5 metres) long.

that drift with the waves.

Anemones are animals without bones that look like plants. They are often home to clown fish. A coating on the clown fish protects it from the anemone's stinging tentacles. The tentacles protect the clown fish and the anemone by keeping predators away.

A skeleton helps a speedy shark swim.

Sharks have endoskeletons made of cartilage. Cartilage is lighter and more flexible than bone, which helps sharks swim fast. Sharks have many rows of teeth that are hard like human teeth. When a shark loses a tooth, another tooth from the row behind moves forward to take its place. Sharks lose and replace thousands of teeth in a lifetime.

Fish shine down deep

Many animals live in the cold dark water thousands of feet below the ocean surface. Some of these creatures, with bones and some without, glow as they illuminate the water for protection or to find food.

where the light is dim.

Many animals live in the water and on land. Some, like seals, are vertebrates with bone skeletons. Others, like crabs, are invertebrates with an exoskeleton. A turtle actually has a shell and a bone endoskeleton and is a vertebrate.

**Skeletons or not,
there is much life to see.**

They all live together

Jelly

Hammerhead
Shark

Blue Whale

Scientists have listed hundreds of thousands
of species that live in the oceans. They believe
there may be millions more to be discovered.

Sea
Stars

in the salty sea.

Eel

Seal

Sunfish

Oarfish

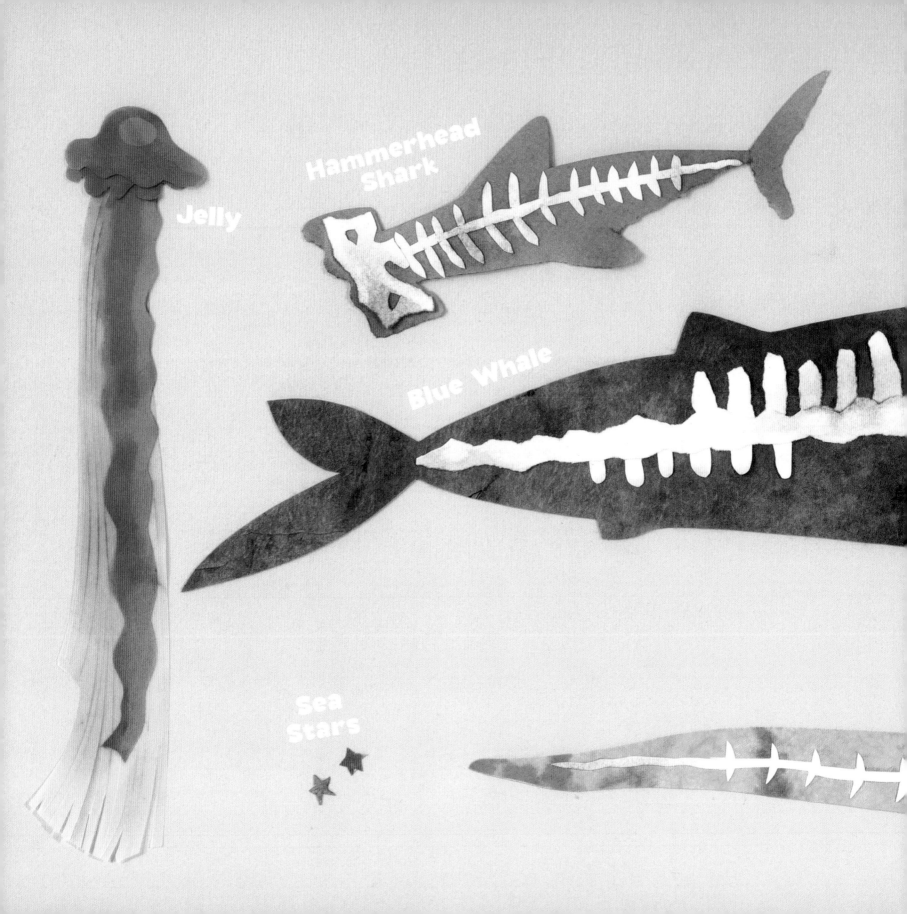

Jelly

Hammerhead
Shark

Blue Whale

Sea
Stars

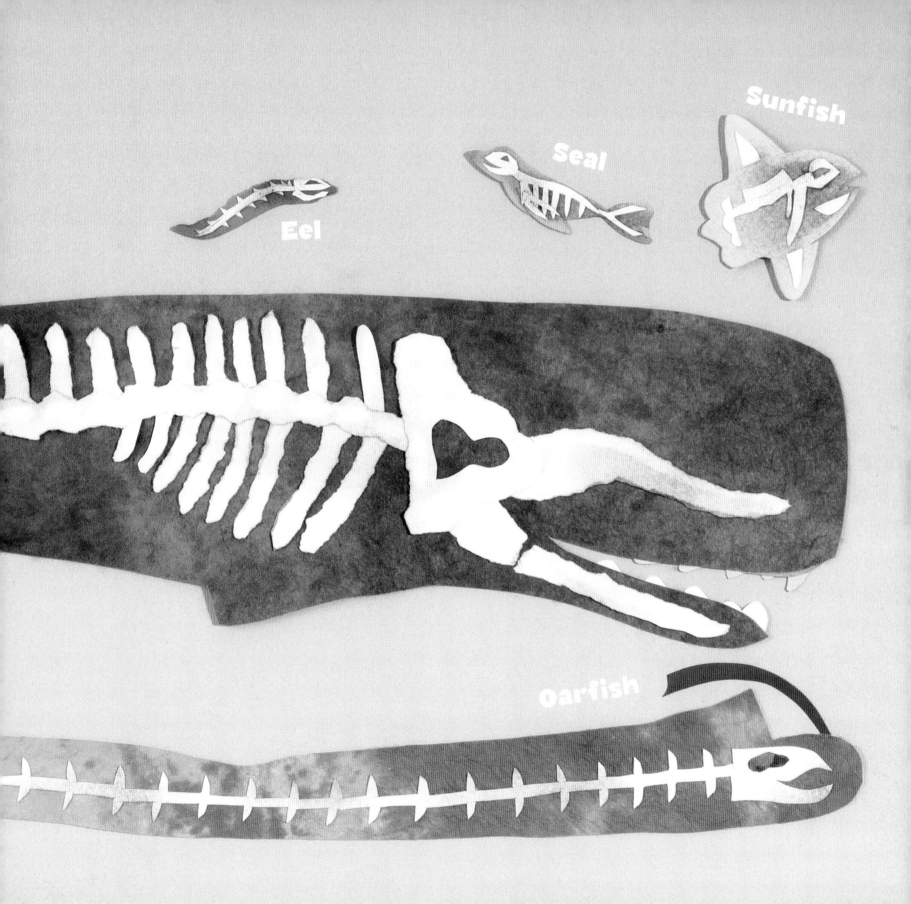

Eel

Seal

Sunfish

Oarfish

Sea Facts

	Jelly	Anglerfish	Ray
Is it a fish?	No	Yes	Yes
Does it have a backbone?	No Invertebrate	Yes Vertebrate	Yes Vertebrate
What kind of skeleton?	No Skeleton	Endoskeleton	Endoskeleton
What does it eat?	Shrimp, Crabs, Fish	Fish, Crustaceans	Plankton, Fish, Mollusks, Crustaceans

Seal	Anemone	Crab	Octopus	Clown Fish
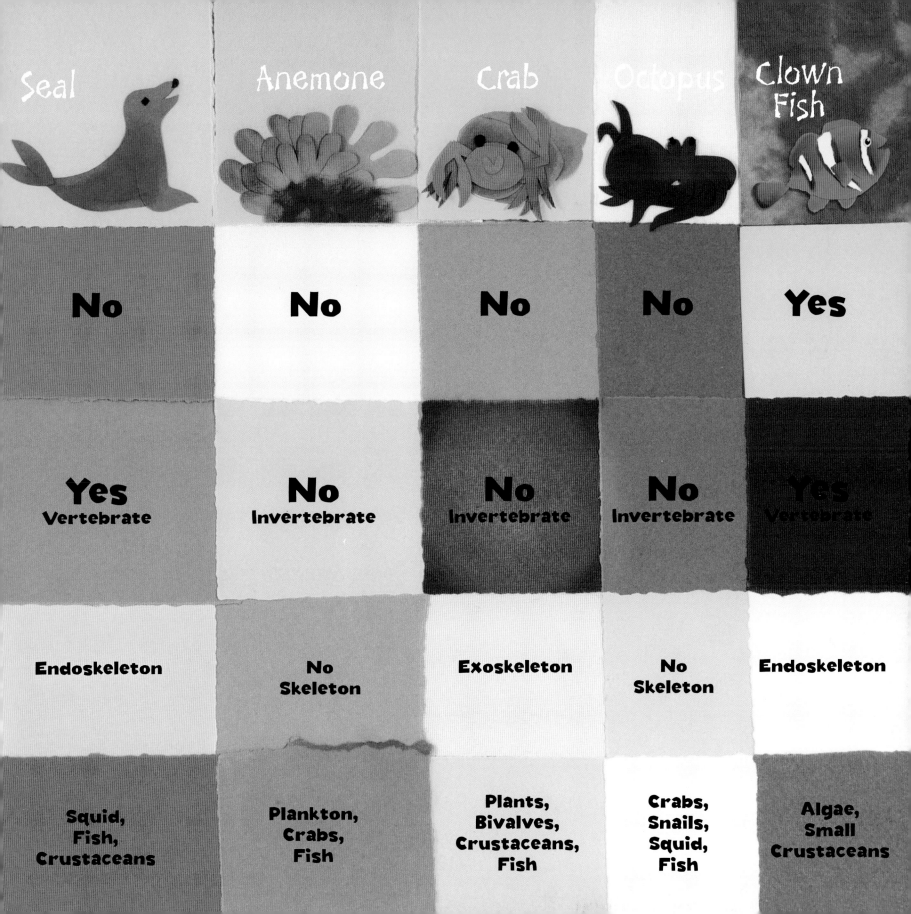				
No	No	No	No	Yes
Yes Vertebrate	No Invertebrate	No Invertebrate	No Invertebrate	Yes Vertebrate
Endoskeleton	No Skeleton	Exoskeleton	No Skeleton	Endoskeleton
Squid, Fish, Crustaceans	Plankton, Crabs, Fish	Plants, Bivalves, Crustaceans, Fish	Crabs, Snails, Squid, Fish	Algae, Small Crustaceans